EWAN McGREGOR

An Unofficial Biography

Written by Martin Noble

A Funfax Book

Ewan McGregor

DK Australia
PO Box 414
St. Leonards
NSW 1590
Australia

DK Publishing, Inc.
95 Madison Avenue
New York, NY 10016

Key: c=centre; t=top; b=bottom; l=left; r=right; a=above

All Action Alan Davidson 34, 36cl, Jonathan Furnics 22cla, Lucy 35cr
Famous Fred Duval 26, Paul Brookes 12, 30
PA News David Giles 29, Rebecca Naden 40
Retna Pictures Ltd Armando Gallo 16, Graig Barritt 3, 11, 23, 48cb, Paul Treadway 37, Steve Granitz 24, SWIRC 9cr, Theodore Wood 21
Rex Features 1c, 18cla, Alistair Devine 7, 33, J. Sutton Hibbert 39, Ken McKay 15, Richard Young 43cr, T. Maitland Titterton 27cr
Frank Spooner Pictures Benainous-Duclos 19cb

Front Cover: **Retna Pictures Ltd** Beneteau/MPA

EWAN McGREGOR
PROFILE LOG

Full name:	Ewan Gordon McGregor
Date of birth:	March 31, 1971
Star sign:	Aries
Birthplace:	Crieff, Scotland, U.K.
Current residence:	London
Height:	5 feet 10 inches
Education:	Morrison's Academy, Crieff
Parents:	Jim McGregor and Carol McGregor
Uncle:	Denis Lawson
Wife:	Eve McGregor (née Mavrakis)
Daughter:	Clara Mathilde McGregor
Hair:	fair
Eyes:	blue
Likes:	family, friends, movies, motorcycles

Best qualities:	loyalty, charm, friendliness, genuineness, sense of fun, energy, drive
Vices:	"naughtiness" (according to Danny Boyle), stubbornness, rebelliousness
Likes to watch:	*ER*; old movies, especially by Frank Capra and starring James Stewart
Likes to read:	anything about James Joyce
Likes to listen to:	Oasis
Likes the sport of:	golf
Likes to play:	guitar, drums
Ewan as a child:	confident, happy, mischievous
Little-known fact:	Ewan's dream is to ride alone on his motorcycle through Europe and Africa
Biggest wishes:	to "go through everything together" with Eve, to make good movies with people he knows and trusts, to help revitalize the British film industry

Definitive Ewan website:

Ewanspotting: The Original Unofficial Ewan McGregor Website

http://www.geocities.com/~ewanmcgregor/main.html

Ewan McGregor Fan Club:

http://members.aol.com/bluevinyl/clubinfo.html

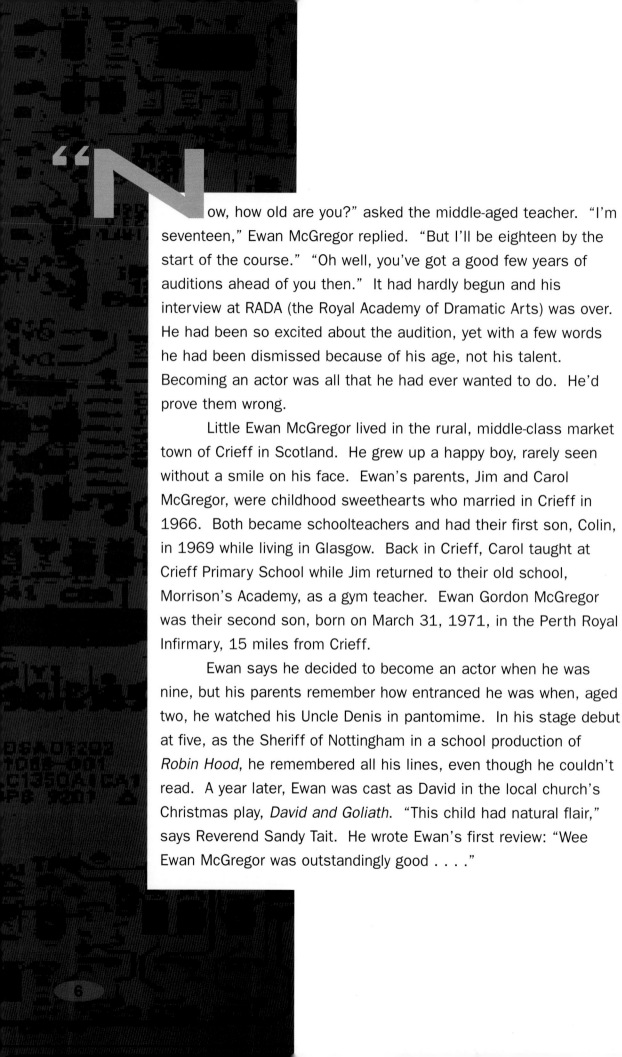

"Now, how old are you?" asked the middle-aged teacher. "I'm seventeen," Ewan McGregor replied. "But I'll be eighteen by the start of the course." "Oh well, you've got a good few years of auditions ahead of you then." It had hardly begun and his interview at RADA (the Royal Academy of Dramatic Arts) was over. He had been so excited about the audition, yet with a few words he had been dismissed because of his age, not his talent. Becoming an actor was all that he had ever wanted to do. He'd prove them wrong.

Little Ewan McGregor lived in the rural, middle-class market town of Crieff in Scotland. He grew up a happy boy, rarely seen without a smile on his face. Ewan's parents, Jim and Carol McGregor, were childhood sweethearts who married in Crieff in 1966. Both became schoolteachers and had their first son, Colin, in 1969 while living in Glasgow. Back in Crieff, Carol taught at Crieff Primary School while Jim returned to their old school, Morrison's Academy, as a gym teacher. Ewan Gordon McGregor was their second son, born on March 31, 1971, in the Perth Royal Infirmary, 15 miles from Crieff.

Ewan says he decided to become an actor when he was nine, but his parents remember how entranced he was when, aged two, he watched his Uncle Denis in pantomime. In his stage debut at five, as the Sheriff of Nottingham in a school production of *Robin Hood*, he remembered all his lines, even though he couldn't read. A year later, Ewan was cast as David in the local church's Christmas play, *David and Goliath*. "This child had natural flair," says Reverend Sandy Tait. He wrote Ewan's first review: "Wee Ewan McGregor was outstandingly good . . . ."

If Ewan inherited his acting talent, it came from his mother's side of the family. Carol's brother Denis Lawson—Ewan's uncle—went to drama school in Glasgow. After performing in a repertory company, he moved to London in the early 1970s. For Ewan, aged seven, the excitement of seeing his Uncle Denis in the role of fighter pilot Wedge Antilles in *Star Wars* was tremendous.

Ewan had always admired Denis, who was often on TV. When his uncle returned to Crieff, he would arrive in a Cadillac. He had long hair, big sideburns, and hippie clothes. "He gave people flowers," says Ewan. "He was an extraordinary character . . . . I wanted to be different like him." "They were a real duo," his father recalls, "always clowning around."

Along with the rest of Crieff, Ewan went to see *Star Wars*—and fell in love with Princess Leia. His school friend Alastair Maclachan, who had a *Star Wars* shrine in his attic, says, "It is quite amazing to think that the boy who used to come round to my house to play with all that stuff is to be a face on the new figures."

ON AMBITION:
"I am very ambitious. I always wanted to be an actor. I took no notice of people who tried to put me off."

The McGregors moved to a Victorian house in a tree-lined lane. Called The Hermitage, it had three bedrooms; Ewan's room overlooked the large back garden. At five, Ewan entered Morrison's Academy primary school. His first years there were happy, and his confidence grew. As a teenager he was always popular. He shone creatively, especially in music, playing drums in the school's Scottish pipe band and with a local ceilidh (folk music) group; he won a prize for mastering the French horn; he learned to play guitar; and he drummed in a short-lived rock group, Scarlet Pride, that split up when he left school.

Ewan's first TV appearance was with the school band. During the show, he wiped his nose on his sleeve in between playing passages from Mozart on the French horn. The cameras tried to avoid him by cutting to closeups of the pianist! He sang well and was in the school choir, winning a prize for a vocal duet with his brother Colin.

When he wasn't at school, Ewan cleaned out stables, learned to ride horses, and enjoyed sub-aqua diving and swimming (which later helped in an underwater scene in *Trainspotting*). He also waited on tables at the Murraypark Hotel. Saturdays were spent watching ancient black-and-white movies. Yvonne McIldowie, who sat next to him in chemistry, remembers Ewan saying that someday he'd be James Bond. "It was intended as a bit of a joke, of course, but you could tell deep down that's what he really wanted," she says.

In 1985, the Queen visited Morrison's for its 125th anniversary. "We did a revue to mark the anniversary, and it was lots of fun," Ewan's friend Alastair recalls. "Ewan came up on stage and did a long poem on his own. Everyone else was having a laugh, but he was taking it very seriously . . . . He was very professional, very confident, very good."

Although Ewan shone in music and drama, in traditional subjects—English, mathematics, and science—he was considered average. At 15, he began experiencing the stresses of the approaching Scottish national exams, the O grades. As these pressures increased, Ewan became restless and confused. He admits he "went off the rails" for a while. "I didn't realize it at the time, but apparently I was."

After passing four O grades (the basic level exams of the Scottish Certificate of Education), Ewan pleaded with his parents to let him leave school to pursue acting. "I felt I had something to live up to a bit," he says of Colin, who became an RAF fighter pilot. "But there was no pressure from anyone." Carol finally relented, realizing Ewan "would be far happier and get on better if he just left and got a job." "She was right," he says. "It was a really brave decision for them to make . . . . They were cool about this crisis and that was a huge relief." There was one proviso: Ewan had to apply to a vocational college. Few said anything to Ewan's face about his decision, but many thought he was crazy. One of his closest friends, Malcolm Copland, apparently told him so, triggering a bust-up between the pair.

ON "BAILING OUT" OF SCHOOL:
"I don't regret it at all, no. What I do regret, however, is not having realized that what you are taught in school is maybe valid. I never really made the connection that what you were being taught was useful in any way. I never thought it was, and I was wrong in that respect."

For Ewan, acting offered a challenge—uncertainty, risk, and escape from Crieff. He had been sullen and moody in his final school year, but remained focused on his goal. As his father says, "From the moment he could walk he always wanted to be an actor." From the age of 14, Ewan had hounded Perth Repertory Theatre. Finally, two weeks after leaving school, he got a part as an extra in *A Passage to India*, which involved "running around the stage with a turban on."

The director of Perth Repertory Theatre offered Ewan a job as a stagehand. He was soon assembling stage sets with the rest of the crew, and stood out for his constant questioning of actors, directors, and stage crew. "Ewan was a good laugh," says Ian Grieve, a crew member. "He was quiet and tended to keep himself to himself, but he wasn't antisocial . . . . He was good at the job, and willing to learn what he didn't know . . . . He enjoyed himself while he was working, and the other lads enjoyed his company . . . . He was very down-to-earth."

The job was poorly paid, involving hard, physical work, but the benefits outweighed the disadvantages for those who wanted to learn the trade. Perth Repertory gave Ewan the experience he needed to secure a place on one of only two foundation drama courses in Scotland. With only 26 places available at Kircaldy College of Technology, he was competing with 200 other applicants. But lecturers were so impressed by his ability to express himself that Ewan won a place on the one-year course.

Aged 17, Ewan left home in August 1988. "I loved Crieff," he says, "but it's the kind of place I eventually wanted to leave." In spite of his tiny cubicle room at Kircaldy, in what one student described as "the worst building I've ever seen in my life," Ewan settled in. He soon impressed the codirector of drama, Lynn Bains. "From the minute he walked in the door he was enthusiastic, willing to do anything you threw at him," she says. "He was talented and very hard-working."

ON SCHOOL:
"I had a great love for music and art, but they don't really let you do that. They think you are copping out, which was a shame. That basically knocked it on the head for me. I became less interested."

Students were put through an intense nine months of training. "If anyone was going to do well on the course," says close college friend Paul Kininmonth, "I reckoned at the time it would be him. He was so confident. He shone in everything he did." In a final exam, Ewan played Batman in a slapstick routine, sending everyone into hysterics.

At 5 feet 10 inches tall, Ewan was now a handsome young man. "Ewan was a great guy," says Kininmonth. "I think girls chased him quite a bit . . . . We were envious of how well Ewan did." Ewan became romantically involved with classmate Hannah Titley. A pretty brunette, Hannah was aiming to go into stage management—hence Ewan's involvement in stage management for most of the class's productions. At the end of the course, with Ewan hoping to continue his studies in London, and Hannah to complete her training in Edinburgh, they pledged to stay together, though separated by 400 miles.

Shortly after his rejection by RADA, Ewan had another chance to prove himself, when he was selected for an interview at the Guildhall School of Music and Drama in London—one of the country's leading training colleges. Winning through preliminary auditions at which he had to sing, he was invited back for the final audition of 100 students that lasted for over two days. The tests were demanding—Ewan was even asked to portray a rubber band. His improvisation impressed the staff, and he was among the first of the 26 successful candidates.

That summer, between finishing at Kircaldy and beginning at Guildhall, Ewan and Hannah rented a flat in Edinburgh, and he worked in a pizzeria. When Ewan left for London they vowed to keep the relationship going.

Coming from Crieff, with its population of 6,000, Ewan found London a complete shock with its crowded streets and high living costs. To see green fields, he had to make a two-hour journey. He lived in a YMCA hostel, a short walk away from the Barbican Arts Centre where the Guildhall is located.

The three-year course was designed to challenge students. Classes ranged from voice techniques to stage fighting, and all the students were encouraged to open up and express themselves.

Initially lacking in self-confidence, Ewan turned to Hannah for reassurance. They spent hours on the telephone—some weekends he went back to Scotland—but after his first year it was clear that they were growing apart, and they decided to split up. "It was a mutual decision," says a friend. "They remain close friends now."

Friends remember Ewan being broke most of the time—he even sold his beloved VW Beetle to raise extra cash. With a college friend he busked at a nearby Underground station, and played in a restaurant on Sundays.

*ON BEING
A SEX SYMBOL:
"It's like asking,
'do you think of
yourself as a sexy
person?' I don't
waste my time
imagining myself
as these things."*

EWAN

The highlight of his second year at the Guildhall was a European tour, including Istanbul and Hamburg, during which Ewan played Orlando in *As You Like It*. "That boosted my confidence quite a lot," he says, "because I had always been scared of Shakespeare."

By 1992, in his third year, staff members noticed how Ewan's natural talent had improved after the rigorous training. "Ewan attracted a lot of interest," says one staff member. "He was good. He always had a very strong presence and a very good rapport with audiences." After his final year's showcase performance, he was approached by Lindy King, his agent to this day. Now Ewan's big chance arrived. He was about to be offered a lead role in a major TV series.

Ewan's party piece, miming to Elvis Presley's "*Hound Dog*," won him his first major role. As the producer and the choreographer of Dennis Potter's new UK drama series, *Lipstick On Your Collar*, watched him dance and mouth the words, they knew that they'd found their Mick Hopper—a bored soldier in the War Office, longing for fame and fortune in 1950s London. "I knew I had found the man," producer Rosemarie Whitman recalls. "We sat there and thought he was just brilliant." Ewan wasn't even required to do a screen test. In early March, a few weeks before the end of his course, he left the Guildhall, encouraged by his teachers.

The seven-month shoot began in March 1992. Playwright Dennis Potter had become one of Britain's most celebrated TV dramatists. In *Lipstick On Your Collar*, he used his trademark musical sequences, with actors miming to records—allowing Ewan to show what he could do. For his role, 20-year-old Ewan McGregor had his hair, eyebrows, and eyelashes dyed jet black. "He was very scruffy when he arrived," the makeup artist recalls. "He was all mousy and spotty, so we did a bit of a transformation. We got the hair curlers on his head, the face packs on, and he loved it."

ON DRAMA SCHOOL: *"I always thought I was fantastic until I got to drama school, where that notion was soundly thrashed out."*

As usual, Ewan paid attention to all aspects of the production, seeking advice from more experienced actors. His moment of glory came when his parents visited Twickenham Studios and Dennis Potter treated them to a meal. Since leaving school, Ewan had had a nagging feeling that he had let his parents down. Their pride helped rid him of those doubts.

Ewan's performance as Hopper was impressive for a beginner, but *Lipstick's* screening was an anticlimax. After months of publicity work for the serial, the media's reaction was poor—although 5 million viewers tuned in.

Ewan McGregor almost went unnoticed. He eagerly looked forward to the serial's TV premiere on February 1, 1993, but the press's lack of interest disappointed him. His fears that he might never work again soon vanished, though. After a month in Morocco acting a small part (two lines) in his first feature film, *Being Human*, he landed a role in a stage play.

In early 1993, Ewan was cast as Nick in Joe Orton's *What the Butler Saw*, at the Salisbury Playhouse. "I had to do two streaks across the stage," he remembers. "To me, being on stage naked is like swimming. It feels really comfortable." That's fortunate, because the role that would reestablish his confidence and advance his career also required him to appear undressed— this time before a much bigger audience. It came with the audition for an epic new BBC costume drama, based on a classic French novel, *Le Rouge et Le Noir* ("Scarlet and Black").

nce director Ben Bolt and producer Ros Wolfes had auditioned Ewan and seen extracts from *Lipstick*, they knew he was perfect for swashbuckling hero Julien Sorel in *Scarlet and Black*. Before filming began, Ewan suffered self-doubts, but these soon disappeared. "Once I put on my military uniform and we started filming in France, everything fell into place."

Some critics felt Ewan was just too handsome for the toy-boy figure of Julien, but 10 million viewers loved *Scarlet and Black*. Ewan, tasting stardom for the first time, was besieged by fan mail, mainly from females.

In the aftermath of *Scarlet and Black*, Ros Wolfes received a call from director Danny Boyle. Why hadn't she asked him to direct the serial? She reminded him that he had been busy doing other things. "OK, tell me about Ewan McGregor," Boyle said. He was looking for an actor to play the lead role in a film about three Edinburgh flatmates, a dead body, and a stack of money.

Shallow Grave was the brainchild of John Hodge, a doctor and screenwriter. After a dozen rewrites, Hodge and producer Andrew Macdonald persuaded the Scottish Film Production Fund to contribute £4,000 toward the project. In January 1993, David Aukin, the head of drama for Britain's Channel 4—an influential television network that also funds and produces feature films—called to arrange a meeting: he liked the script he'd read and Channel 4 would back the movie.

As the dream of creating a new type of upbeat British thriller began to take shape, Hodge and Macdonald looked for a director to share their vision. Director Danny Boyle says, "When I read it I thought it was a really exciting script—clean and mean and truly cinematic." While Robert Carlyle (later to star in *The Full Monty* and *Trainspotting*) had auditioned for the part of wisecracking journalist Alex Law, Ewan finally won the part.

The intensive shoot lasted 30 days. In the movie, three flatmates gradually turn against each other after discovering a suitcase full of cash in the room of their murdered lodger. After its first showing at the Cannes Film Festival in May 1994, the reaction to *Shallow Grave* was sensational. British audiences eagerly awaited its release, which was to come in January 1995. Meanwhile, Ewan, hailed as one of the great new acting talents of British movies, was preparing for another dramatic change in his life.

Ewan fell for Eve Mavrakis on the set of *Kavanagh QC*, a new legal drama series, when he was playing a student and she was assistant art director. "When she met Ewan," says Eve's sister Marianne, "she felt very, very strongly that he was the man for her. She knew deep down he was the love of her life. . . ." The couple married in July 1995 in the Dordogne, France—Eve's homeland.

ON THE BRITISH FILM INDUSTRY: *"We have got really good writers here, incredible facilities, the best technicians in the world, and we make really good movies. The quality of our work is far superior."*

wan was not looking his best. He had just finished shooting *Trainspotting*, for which he had had a skinhead haircut and lost two stone (28 pounds) to play heroin addict Mark Renton. Eve looked radiant, though. "It was a wonderful wedding, just the way they wanted," says Jim McGregor. "But he was the most nervous person I have ever seen when he was doing his speech."

While working on *Kavanagh QC*, Ewan shot two other films, neither of which were high profile. In *Doggin' Around*, a BBC comedy drama about an American jazz pianist, Ewan plays a bass player. It was an enjoyable part in a well-received film. *Blue Juice*, Ewan's last 1994 project, was his biggest so far. At £2 million (about $3.3 million), the film's budget (raised by Channel 4) was double that for *Shallow Grave*. A surfing movie based in Cornwall, England, Ewan played hippie Dean Raymond. "I had a great time filming in Cornwall for ten weeks. . . . I've never partied so much in my life." The movie was not a great success, as Ewan admits: "It's a bit muddled in the middle, it's just a shame, it's not really very good."

He had no need to worry. *Shallow Grave* had become the biggest British movie of the year, and director Danny Boyle, producer Andrew Macdonald, and screenwriter John Hodge were besieged by Hollywood. "We've been taken out to lunch by Disney, by Fox—we've had some crazy offers," said Macdonald. But they were already planning their next project.

ON WIFE EVE:
"I knew from the very first day I saw her. She's beautiful, so beautiful. The second I saw her I thought if I could be with her it would be like nothing I've ever had before."

ndrew Macdonald had first read Irvine Welsh's book *Trainspotting* in December 1993 after the *Shallow Grave* shoot. He'd read it while flying home to Scotland, where the novel had achieved cult status. While the subject matter seemed bleak—revolving around drug addicts in 1980s Edinburgh—the book was gripping. Macdonald knew it would make a great movie. Once Boyle had been persuaded, they had to convince Hodge, who told them that it was amazing but would never make a film. They refused to take no for an answer, and over Christmas 1994 Hodge completed a draft.

Mark Renton, the most entertaining character, became the central focus of the movie. There was no contest about who would play him. Macdonald and Boyle gave Ewan the script at the Sundance Festival, where they were promoting *Shallow Grave*. "Ewan was a logical choice," says Boyle. "Ewan has phenomenal technical skill which allows him to use the camera to its full extent. He's actually not the most gorgeous-looking person . . . but there's something about him that's attractive because he's more human. He has that slight edge of the boy next door." Ewan described the role as "a million birthday presents."

Losing weight for the part was no problem for Ewan. He began his diet a few months early, while filming Peter Greenaway's *The Pillow Book*, and told his friends to watch the film closely and they would see he was thinner at the end of the movie than at the beginning. In *The Pillow Book*, a fantasy based on a tenth-century text, Ewan plays a translator who accidentally kills himself, is buried, dug up, and turned into a book. Shot in Luxembourg, Hong Kong, and Japan in 1994–95, the film has virtually no dialogue. Ewan describes the script as one of the most beautiful he has seen. Released in Britain in 1996 after *Trainspotting*, it was a critical success. "McGregor shows that he is one of the cinema's boldest, most charming young actors," wrote *Time* magazine.

EWAN

But it was *Trainspotting*—with Ewan, wet and skeleton-like, appearing on billboard advertisements—that launched him in 1996 as the face of the revived British movie scene. *Trainspotting* tells the story of Renton and his friends Spud, Sick Boy, Tommy, and Begbie—a group of young drug addicts. Ewan has never taken drugs and never intends to. He researched his character thoroughly, reading every book he could find on drug abuse and talking to addicts. Brilliantly filmed, the movie speeds along and is very funny yet terribly sad. With a memorable soundtrack and superb acting, it was an instant hit, despite the controversial subject matter. The magazine *Empire* described it as "the movie of the decade." Now no one could deny Ewan's star status. "I'm so proud of the film," he has said, "because I think we told the truth, I think we showed the way it is."

Ewan's career was rocketing. His next move was to star in Douglas McGrath's film of the classic Jane Austen novel *Emma*. Possibly because of the pressure, or maybe uncomfortable in the role of Frank Churchill—Emma's smooth, untrustworthy suitor—Ewan gave his worst performance yet. "I think the film's all right but I . . . was terrible in it," says Ewan. "I didn't believe a word I said . . . I was really embarrassed about it . . . ." He thinks he concentrated so hard on his English accent that he forgot everything else. "It's all right to do a bad one," he adds. "We'll move on." He did—straight to the former mining village of Grimethorpe to film *Brassed Off*.

Brassed Off is a black comedy, bleak but often funny, about a Yorkshire colliery brass band. As the local mine faces closure, the band struggles to stay together and carry on to a national competition final. Ewan plays the part of Andy, a young miner and trumpet player. Along with Pete Postlethwaite, Stephen Tompkinson, and Tara Fitzgerald, Ewan gives one of his best performances, and the movie received great critical acclaim.

Despite growing fame and admiration in 1996, with the release of *Trainspotting, Emma*, *The Pillow Book*, and *Brassed Off*, the most important event in Ewan's life was in February, when his wife Eve gave birth to their daughter, Clara Mathilde McGregor.

After Clara's birth, Ewan returned alone to their flat to ring family and friends. While still a bachelor in 1992, Ewan had rented the stylish flat in Primrose Hill—a sophisticated area of north London. But now that he had a family, and could afford it, he bought a townhouse near St. John's Wood for a reported £1.25 million (about $2 million). He and Eve hired architects, and began converting the house into their home.

When not filming or promoting his latest movie, Ewan devoted himself to his new family, played the occasional round of golf, and enjoyed going out. At the beginning of 1997 he took a three-month break; this time turned into the worst period of his life, when Clara developed meningitis. Fortunately she made a complete recovery. The experience helped Ewan to put success into perspective. "The best thing about the year," he recalls, "was my baby coming through that. It's the scariest thing that has ever happened, and the happiest."

Eve and Clara go everywhere with Ewan, even on film sets—he has this written into his contract. "He's a really good daddy. He's also a really good husband," says Eve's sister, Marianne. "Eve and Ewan love each other dearly. On one occasion she was working in Kenya on a shoot. He loved her so much he flew out to be with her because he could not bear to spend a weekend away from her."

ON THE BIRTH OF HIS DAUGHTER CLARA: *"I phoned a lot of people, crying down the phone to my parents. . . ."*

EWAN

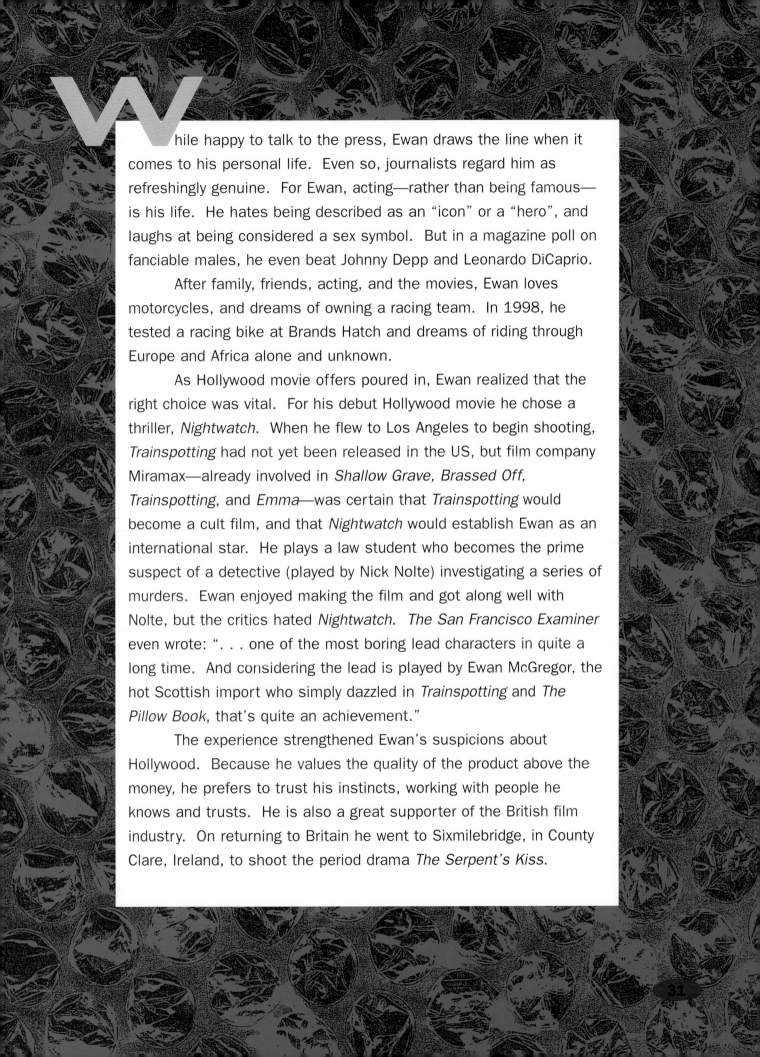

While happy to talk to the press, Ewan draws the line when it comes to his personal life. Even so, journalists regard him as refreshingly genuine. For Ewan, acting—rather than being famous—is his life. He hates being described as an "icon" or a "hero", and laughs at being considered a sex symbol. But in a magazine poll on fanciable males, he even beat Johnny Depp and Leonardo DiCaprio.

After family, friends, acting, and the movies, Ewan loves motorcycles, and dreams of owning a racing team. In 1998, he tested a racing bike at Brands Hatch and dreams of riding through Europe and Africa alone and unknown.

As Hollywood movie offers poured in, Ewan realized that the right choice was vital. For his debut Hollywood movie he chose a thriller, *Nightwatch*. When he flew to Los Angeles to begin shooting, *Trainspotting* had not yet been released in the US, but film company Miramax—already involved in *Shallow Grave, Brassed Off, Trainspotting*, and *Emma*—was certain that *Trainspotting* would become a cult film, and that *Nightwatch* would establish Ewan as an international star. He plays a law student who becomes the prime suspect of a detective (played by Nick Nolte) investigating a series of murders. Ewan enjoyed making the film and got along well with Nolte, but the critics hated *Nightwatch*. *The San Francisco Examiner* even wrote: ". . . one of the most boring lead characters in quite a long time. And considering the lead is played by Ewan McGregor, the hot Scottish import who simply dazzled in *Trainspotting* and *The Pillow Book*, that's quite an achievement."

The experience strengthened Ewan's suspicions about Hollywood. Because he values the quality of the product above the money, he prefers to trust his instincts, working with people he knows and trusts. He is also a great supporter of the British film industry. On returning to Britain he went to Sixmilebridge, in County Clare, Ireland, to shoot the period drama *The Serpent's Kiss*.

Set in Gloucestershire in 1699, Ewan plays Meneer Chrome, a Dutch landscape gardener who is chased by the wife of his employer, Thomas Smithers (Pete Postlethwaite), while falling in love with Smithers's daughter. "It was a very relaxed shoot, but hard work at the same time," says producer Robert Jones. Jones praised Ewan for his commitment to the project. "He committed a good six to eight months before the film was shot. In that time there were a lot of people after him for other things. He stayed very true to it." "I'm passionate about it," Ewan said of the script. "It's one of the best I've read in a long time and it's beautifully written."

While all this was going on, Boyle, Macdonald, and Hodge had come up with a third project for Ewan. In *A Life Less Ordinary*, Ewan plays Robert, a Scotsman who cleans offices for a living. After being fired, he kidnaps his boss's spoiled daughter (Cameron Diaz) and robs a bank.

The film almost didn't happen; Danny Boyle had been tempted by Hollywood to direct the fourth Alien movie, *Alien Resurrection*. But as Macdonald says, "After a few meetings, Danny and I realized *Alien 4* wasn't the kind of film we wanted to do." The Figment Films crew who made *Shallow Grave* and *Trainspotting* were a team, and Ewan was part of it. "No question, he's part of our core team," says Macdonald. Ewan feels the same about them, especially Boyle. "He's the best there is, that's it," he says. "I've never felt happier working with anyone else." "Ewan's a mate," says Danny. "He's also the best film actor in Britain at the moment . . . ."

The same executives who had offered the team *Alien Resurrection* agreed to back Channel 4's initial funds for *A Life Less Ordinary*. Sean Connery was offered a cameo role as God,

but unfortunately he declined. He had other commitments, but told Macdonald how much he'd enjoyed *Trainspotting*.

Cameron Diaz became Ewan's kidnap victim. "I didn't know the chemistry would be there between us, but it was, luckily," says Ewan. "Because from day one, it was obvious that we were going to have a good time. . . . You can see it in our eyes that we're genuinely enjoying each other's company." Diaz returns the compliments. "In the film I fall in love with Ewan's character," she says. "And you can see how any girl could fall for him in real life, too."

Cameron and Ewan became good friends, and the chemistry between them was great publicity for the movie. As usual, Eve and Clara joined him in Utah (Eve worked on the film as designer) and Ewan was fond of saying, "It's very nice to kiss Cameron Diaz, but it doesn't give me any concern about when I get home to my wife because it's work. It's not work, of course, kissing Cameron," he added jokingly. Sadly, the film was criticized as having a confused plot and was voted 1997's third biggest flop.

The publicity people promoting Ewan in the US had arranged for him to appear as a guest star on America's most popular TV series, *ER*. In the episode—*The Long Way Around*, screened in February 1997—Duncan (Ewan) robs a store. When his accomplice is shot by the store owner, he panics, shoots the owner, injures several customers, and takes everyone in the store hostage. *ER*'s Nurse Hathaway (Julianna Margulies), a customer, wins his trust during the siege. Duncan eventually flees, is shot by a cop, and dies on the operating table. Ewan's performance won him an Emmy nomination for Outstanding Guest Appearance on a Drama Series.

ollowing Clara's recovery from meningitis, Ewan returned to work in March 1997 to film *Velvet Goldmine*. He plays Curt Wild, a 1970s glam rock star. While preparing for his first big scene, a telephone call sent his mind whirring back to when he was a boy in Crieff. His agent, Lindy King, had phoned: he was to play Obi-Wan Kenobi in George Lucas's new *Star Wars* trilogy. Just like his Uncle Denis, Ewan was to be in *Star Wars!* And not just as a fighter pilot, but in the role that Alec Guinness had made famous in 1977. His childhood dream had come true! The worst thing about it—the only drawback—was that Ewan was sworn to secrecy. "It was quite a day, knowing I got it and not being able to tell anyone. It was hard."

Ewan was not permitted to say anything for two whole months. For the time being he had to focus on *Velvet Goldmine*. Curt Wild was a challenging role, but it allowed him to play out his young dreams of becoming a rock star. It also showed how versatile he is, as Wild undergoes a series of transformations. While Ewan has never been into the glam rock revival ("It all seems a bit sad to me"), he admits that he is fascinated with the idea of being a rock star. He has been an Oasis fan since their first album, when he met them.

EWAN

Though *Velvet Goldmine* received only a minor award at Cannes, over time it may come to be seen as a great movie. Now it was time for Ewan to go even farther into space and time.

The news in 1994 that George Lucas was writing screenplays for three *Star Wars* prequels (films showing events that happen before those in the original) thrilled fans around the world. "If they ask you, 'Do you want to be Obi-Wan Kenobi?', you just cannot say no," Ewan says.

At £40 million (about $67 million), the budget for the film in which Ewan stars was relatively small. But in May 1996, Pepsi paid a record-breaking £1.2 billion ($2 billion) for merchandising, and in 1997 the biggest-ever toy licensing agreement was made to create toys for the new movies, including Ewan McGregor action figures.

Filming the new *Star Wars* movie in Britain was top secret. Ewan, like everyone else, had to sign a contract not to speak about casting or production. "It was the most secretive operation I've ever seen," agreed one of the construction workers, who spent months building over 50 sets that were dismantled a few days after shooting finished.

For Ewan, just being on the *Star Wars* set was a buzz in itself. "I walked into the props room and there were about 50 prop makers . . . I saw R2-D2 at the end of the room. I just started going, 'Aaaaaaaaaa.'"

Ewan's screen test came in March 1997 with Liam Neeson, who was being screen-tested for the role of the master Jedi who trains the young Kenobi in the ways of the Force. The result confirmed the master/student chemistry that would be so important on screen.

ON VELVET GOLDMINE:
"I wear lots of long bleached-blond wigs, leather trousers, and hipster flares. I'm quite grungy."

ON STAR WARS:
"When you're my age, and you were out there cheering when the first Star Wars came out, what are you going to do when they offer one of the leads in the new film? Say no? No way. Can you imagine what it'll be like sitting down in some screening room, the curtain goes up, and there it is, the new movie? Magic."

Most of Ewan's acting was performed against a blank canvas background, known as a "bluescreen"; it would take another 18 months for all the special effects to be superimposed. "The exciting thing will be seeing it in the preview . . ." Ewan says. "Watching it and seeing what they've put around about you . . . ."

Ewan next headed for Scarborough, England, to begin filming *The Rise and Fall of Little Voice*. A modern-day *Cinderella story*, it focuses on Little Voice (played by Jane Horrocks), a wonderful, but very shy, singer who finds her soulmate in Billy (Ewan), a telephone engineer. As usual, Ewan captivated everyone he worked with. "Ewan was brilliant," said producer Elisabeth Karlsen. "He is a great actor and we loved making the film with him."

No sooner had Ewan finished shooting than he was on to his next movie. Friends felt he was taking on too much. But, as one friend said, he was in such demand as an actor that a film could only get the go-ahead if Ewan committed to it. So nine hours after finishing *Little Voice*, Ewan arrived at Pinewood Studios in London to begin work on *Rogue Trader*.

In *Rogue Trader*, Ewan plays Nick Leeson, a disgraced financial trader. It's a true story about the general manager of the Singapore office of Barings, one of the world's oldest merchant banks. Leeson played the world's markets, but used the bank's money to hide a massive loss. When Barings collapsed with huge debts, Leeson went to prison. Based on Leeson's autobiography, the movie has attracted controversy: some people criticize the fact that a convicted criminal might profit from his crime, although the producers argue that any money Leeson makes will be used up in legal fees.

> *"There's nothing cooler than being a Jedi Knight. It's so familiar wearing all the Jedi stuff, the clogs and the lightsabers. And I'm actually like: 'What is this?' It's part of your childhood, and you're involved in it. It's very weird . . . . The first day I got dressed properly it was quite a moment for a boy from Scotland to stand there and look in the mirror: 'Jedi McGregor.'"*

eeson's wife is played by Anna Friel, best known for her role in the British television soap *Brookside*. She and Ewan became very close while shooting. "We are male and female versions of each other," she says. "His parents are both teachers; so are mine. His brother flies for the RAF; so does mine." When photos of Ewan and Anna kissing appeared in British tabloid newspapers, both were furious. Some had been taken during filming; others were simply the two friends greeting each other. It was the first time Ewan had experienced that kind of press intrusion, and it made him more suspicious of the media.

Arriving home exhausted at the end of January 1998, Ewan decided to take a month off. Although he loves working, he knew this time he had overdone it. Ewan had been on the go virtually nonstop since *Shallow Grave* over four years earlier.

ON TRAINSPOTTING:
"They gave me the script on the understanding there was no presumption that I would be in the film. I read it and thought: 'I've got to play this part.'"

Besides filming, Ewan has recorded voice-overs and even appeared in filmed ads for Japanese TV. His voice from the *Trainspotting* soundtrack was also sampled on a record, "*Choose Life*" by PF Project, which hit number one in the British charts in November 1997.

In December 1997, Ewan, together with actor friends Jude Law, Sadie Frost, Jonny Lee Miller, and Sean Pertwee, and producers Damon Bryant and Bradley Adams, formed the production company Natural Nylon. They have raised £62.5 million ($100 million) to fund ten British-made movies. Nylon's projects include: *eXistenZ*, a cyber thriller to be directed by David Cronenberg; a film about the life of Brian Epstein, the Beatles' manager; an adaptation of Iain Banks's *The Bridge*; a thriller based on the novel *Psychoville*; a movie about the mid-eighteenth-century Hellfire Club, in which Ewan will play the politician John Wilkes; and *Nora*, in which Ewan would play James Joyce in a film about Joyce's wife, Nora Barnacle.

Ewan was back at work in Montreal in spring 1998, to star as a private eye in *Eye of the Beholder*. Directed by Stephen Elliott, who made *Priscilla, Queen of the Desert*, the movie also stars singer k. d. lang. In mid-November 1998, a bearded Ewan McGregor walked out on stage at the Hampstead Theatre Club in London as Malcolm Scrawdyke in the production *Little Malcolm and His Struggle Against the Eunuchs*. "I was depressed one night and I phoned up my Uncle Denis," he recalls. "I said: 'I really want to do a play . . . I want you to direct it because I'm frightened enough about it, and I think it would be nice if you were there."

The play that uncle and nephew chose to do together, with Denis as director, is about an art school rebellion. It was a brave step for Ewan—critics can be hard on film actors who "take to the boards"—but their reaction has been enthusiastic. Denis and Ewan are now planning a film together, *Don't Think Twice*—a rock 'n' roll movie. "We get a chance to sing and play guitar," says Ewan, "which we do together already."

The wheel has turned full circle. The young boy who gazed at his uncle on screen in *Star Wars* back in 1977, and who dreamed of following in his footsteps, has become, maybe reluctantly, an icon for the late 1990s and for the new millennium.

FILMOGRAPHY

Being Human (1993)

Directed by: Bill Forsyth
Written by: Bill Forsyth
Produced by: David Puttnam and Robert G. Colesberry
Music by: Michael Gibbs

Hector	Robin Williams
Lucinnius	John Turturro
Beatrice	Anna Galiena
Priest	Vincent D'Onofrio
Francisco	Jonathan Hyde
Narrator	Theresa Russell
Celtic priest	Robert Carlyle
Alvarez	Ewan McGregor*

Brief appearance

Shallow Grave (1995)

Directed by: Danny Boyle
Written by: John Hodge
Produced by: Andrew Macdonald
Music by: Simon Boswell
Photography by: Brian Tufano

Juliet Miller	Kerry Fox
David Stephens	Christopher Eccleston
Alex Law	Ewan McGregor
Det. Insp. McCall	Ken Stott
Hugo	Keith Allen
Cameron	Colin McCredie
Andy	Peter Mullan
D. C. Mitchell	John Hodge
Would-be Tenant	Carol McGregor

Blue Juice (1995)

Directed by: Carl Prechezer
Written by: Peter Salmi and Carl Prechezer
Produced by: Simon Relph and Peter Salmi
Music by: Simon Davison
Photography by: Richard Greatrex

JC	Sean Pertwee
Chloe	Catherine Zeta Jones
Josh Tambini	Steven Mackintosh
Dean Raymond	Ewan McGregor
Terry Colcott	Peter Gunn
Shaper	Heathcote Williams
Junior	Colette Brown
Mike	Keith Allen

Trainspotting (1996)

Directed by: Danny Boyle
Written by: John Hodge
Based on the novel by: Irvine Welsh
Produced by: Andrew Macdonald
Photography by: Brian Tufano

Renton	Ewan McGregor
Spud	Ewen Bremner
Sick Boy	Jonny Lee Miller
Begbie	Robert Carlyle
Diane	Kelly Macdonald
Tommy	Kevin McKidd
Swanney	Peter Mullan
Mr Renton	James Cosmo
Mrs Renton	Eileen Nicholas
Allison	Susan Vidler

Emma (1996)

Directed by: Douglas McGrath
Written by: Douglas McGrath
Based on the novel by: Jane Austen
Produced by: Steven Haft and Patrick Cassavetti
Photography by: Ian Wilson
Music by: Rachel Portman

Emma Woodhouse	Gwyneth Paltrow
Mr. Knightley	Jeremy Northam
Harriet Smith	Toni Collette
Mr. Elton	Alan Cumming
Mrs. Weston	Greta Scacchi
Mr. Weston	James Cosmo
Miss Bates	Sophie Thompson
Frank Churchill	Ewan McGregor

Brassed Off (1996)

Directed by: Mark Herman
Written by: Mark Herman
Produced by: Steven Abbott
Photography by: Andy Collins
Music by: Trevor Jones

Danny	Pete Postlethwaite
Phil	Stephen Tompkinson
Gloria	Tara Fitzgerald
Andy	Ewan McGregor
Harry	Jim Carter
Greasley	Ken Colley
Simmo	Peter Gunn
Sandra	Melanie Hill

The Pillow Book (1996)

Directed by: Peter Greenaway
Written by: Peter Greenaway
Produced by: Kees Kasander
Photography by: Sacha Vierny

Nagiko	Vivian Wu
The Publisher	Yoshi Oida
The Father	Ken Ogata
The Aunt/The Maid	Hideko Yoshida
Jerome	Ewan McGregor
The Mother	Judy Ongg
The Husband	Ken Mitsuishi
Hoki	Yutaka Honda

A Life Less Ordinary (1997)

Directed by: Danny Boyle
Written by: John Hodge
Produced by: Andrew Macdonald
Photography by: Brian Tufano

Rober	Ewan McGregor
Celine	Cameron Diaz
O'Reilly	Holly Hunter
Jackson	Delroy Lindo
Naville	Ian Holm
Mayhew	Ian McNeice
Elliot	Stanley Tucci
Gabriel	Dan Hedaya

The Serpent's Kiss (1997)

Directed by: Philippe Rousselot
Written by: Tim Rose Price
Produced by: Robert Jones, John Battsek and Tim Rose Price
Photography by: Jean-François Robin
Music by: Goran Bregovic

Meneer Chrome	Ewan McGregor
Juliana	Greta Scacchi
Thomas Smithers	Pete Postlethwaite
Fitzmaurice	Richard E. Grant
Thea	Carmen Chaplin
Physician	Donal McCann
Secretary	Charley Boorman
Mr. Galmoy	Gerard McSorley

Nightwatch (1998)

Directed by: Ole Bornedal
Written by: Ole Bornedal and Steven Soderbergh
Based on the script for Nattevagten by: Ole Bornedal
Produced by: Michael Obel
Photography by: Dan Laustsen
Music by: Joachim Holbek

Martin	Ewan McGregor
Inspector Cray	Nick Nolte
Catherine	Patricia Arquette
James	Josh Brolin
Joyce	Alix Koromzay
Marie	Lauren Graham
Inspector Davis	John C. Reilly
Duty Doctor	Brad Dourif

Velvet Goldmine (1998)

Directed by: Todd Haynes
Written by: Todd Haynes
Story by: Todd Haynes amd James Lyons
Produced by: Christine Vachon
Photography by: Maryse Alberti
Music by: Carter Burwell

Curt Wild	Ewan McGregor
Brian Slade	Jonathan Rhys-Meyers
Mandy Slade	Toni Collette
Arthur Stuart	Christian Bale
Jerry Divine	Eddie Izzard
Shannon	Emily Woof
Cecil	Michael Feast
Jack Fairy	Micko Westmoreland

Still To Be Released

Star Wars: Episode 1
The Phantom Menace (1999)

Directed by: George Lucas
Written by: George Lucas
Produced by: Rick McCallum
Photography by: David Tattersall

Obi-Wan Kenobi	Ewan McGregor
Anakin Skywalker	Jake Lloyd
Qui-Gon Jinn	Liam Neeson
Padme Naberrie Amidale	Natalie Portman
Mace Windu	Samuel L. Jackson
Chancellor Valorum	Terence Stamp
Senator Palpatine	Ian McDiarmid

The Rise and Fall of Little Voice (aka Little Voice) (1998)

Directed by: Mark Herman
Written by: Mark Herman
Based on the play by: Jim Cartwright
Produced by: Elizabeth Karlsen
Photography by: Andy Collins

Laura Hoff	Jane Horrocks
Ray Say	Michael Caine
Mari Hoff	Brenda Blethyn
Billy	Ewan McGregor
Mr. Boo	Jim Broadbent

Rogue Trader (1998)

Directed by: James Dearden
Written by: James Dearden
Based on the book by: Nick Leeson
Produced by: Paul Raphael, James Dearden and Janette Day
Photography by: Jean-François Robin

Nick Leeson	Ewan McGregor
Lisa Lesson	Anna Friel
Other actors include:	Tom Wu
	Nigel Lindsey
	Irene Ng
	Lee Ross

Eye of the Beholder (1999)

Directed by: Stephan Elliott
Written by: Stephan Elliott
Based on the novel by: Marc Behm
Produced by: Nicolas Clermont and Tony Smith
Photography by: Guy Dufaux

"The Eye"	Ewan McGregor
Hilary	k. d. lang
Other actors include:	Jason Priestley
	Genevieve Bujold
	Ashley Judd

Short Films

Family Style	(1994)
Sleeping With the Fishes	(1996)
Desserts	(1998)

Television Appearances

Lipstick On Your Collar (UK, 1993, six episodes)

Directed by: Renny Rye
Written by: Dennis Potter
Produced by: Dennis Potter
Photography by: Sean Van Hales
Choreography by: Quinny Sacks

Francis Francis	Giles Thomas
Mick Hopper	Ewan McGregor
Sylvia Berry	Louise Germaine
Corporal Peter Berry	Douglas Henshall
Lt. Col. Harry Bernwood	Peter Jeffrey
Major Wallace Hedges	Clive Francis
Major Archie Carter	Nicholas Jones
Major Johnny Church	Nicholas Farrell
Colonel 'Truck' Trekker	Shane Rimmer
Harold Atterbow	Roy Hudd
Aunt Vickie	Maggie Steed
Uncle Fred	Bernard Hill
Lisa	Kymberley Huffman

Scarlet and Black (UK, 1993, three episodes)

Directed by: Ben Bolt
Written by: Stephen Lowe
Based on the novel Le Rouge et le Noir by: Stendhal
Produced by: Rosalind Wolfes
Photography by: John McGlashan
Music by: Jean-Claude Petit

Julien Sorel	Ewan McGregor
Madame de Renal	Alice Krige
Mathilde	Rachel Weisz
Napoleon	Christopher Fulford
Abbe Pirard	Stratford Johns
Marquis de la Mole	T.P. McKenna
Monsieur de Renal	Martin Jarvis
Monsieur Valenod	Michael Attwell

Doggin' Around (UK, 1994)

Directed by: Desmond Davis
Written by: Alan Plater
Produced by: Otto Plaschkes
Photography by: Denis Lewiston

Joe Warren	Elliott Gould
Sarah Williams	Geraldine James
Charlie Foster	Alun Armstrong
Tom Clayton	Ewan McGregor
Mrs. Thompson	Liz Smith
Gary Powell	Anthony Etherton
(Himself)	Ronnie Scott
Pete	Neil McCaul

Kavanagh QC—Nothing But the Truth (UK, 1995)

Directed by: Colin Gregg
Written by: Russell Lewis
Produced by: Chris Kelly
Photography by: Nigel Walters
Music by: Anne Dudley

James Kavanagh	John Thaw
Eleanor Harker	Geraldine James
Eve Kendall	Alison Steadman
David Armstrong	Ewan McGregor
Julia Piper	Anna Chancellor
Sophie	Elli Garnett
Kate Kavanagh	Daisy Bates
Lizzie Kavanagh	Lisa Harrow

Tales from the Crypt—Cold War (US, 1996)

Directed by: Andy Morahan
Written by: Scott Nimerfro
Produced by: Gilbert Adler
Photography by: Robin Vidgeon
Music by: J. Peter Robinson

Ford	Ewan McGregor
Cammy	Jane Horrocks
Other actors include:	Colin Salmon
	John Salthouse
	Willie Ross
	John Kassir

Karaoke (UK, 1997)

Ewan had a walk-on role.

ER—The Long Way Around (US, 1997)

Directed by: Christopher Chulack
Written by: Lydia Woodward
Created by: Michael Crichton
Produced by: Christopher Chulack
Photography by: Richard Thorpe
Music by: Martin Davich

Carol Hathaway	Julianna Margulies
Duncan Stewart	Ewan McGregor
Jerry Markovic	Abraham Benrubi
Robert Potter	Mason Gamble
Dr. Doug Ross	George Clooney
Other actors include:	Currie Graham
	Ruth Maleczech
	Jan Rubes

Stage Appearances

What the Butler Saw (Salisbury Playhouse, UK, 1993)

Nick	Ewan McGregor

Little Malcolm and His Struggle Against the Eunuchs (Hampstead Theatre, London, 1998)

Directed by: Denis Lawson
Written by: David Halliwell

Malcolm Scrawdyke	Ewan McGregor

Radio Dramas

Tragic Prelude	**(1992)**
The Real Thing	**(1992)**

EWAN
McGREGOR